Jelly Roll Jam

Simple Quilts Made with 2½" Strips

Barbara Groves and Mary Jacobson
of *Me and My Sister Designs*

Martingale®
Create with Confidence

Jelly Roll Jam: Simple Quilts Made with 2½" Strips
© 2022 by Barbara Groves and Mary Jacobson

Martingale®
18939 120th Ave. NE, Ste. 101
Bothell, WA 98011-9511 USA
ShopMartingale.com

Printed in Hong Kong
27 26 25 24 23 22   8 7 6 5 4 3 2 1

Library of Congress Cataloging-in-Publication Data
is available upon request.

ISBN: 978-1-68356-172-9

MISSION STATEMENT

We empower makers who use fabric and yarn
to make life more enjoyable.

CREDITS

**PUBLISHER AND
CHIEF VISIONARY OFFICER**
Jennifer Erbe Keltner

CONTENT DIRECTOR
Karen Costello Soltys

TECHNICAL EDITOR
Nancy Mahoney

COPY EDITOR
Sheila Chapman Ryan

ILLUSTRATOR
Sandy Loi

DESIGN MANAGER
Adrienne Smitke

PRODUCTION MANAGER
Regina Girard

**COVER AND
BOOK DESIGNER**
Mia Mar

PHOTOGRAPHER
Brent Kane

Contents

Introduction

We love precuts! We've long been fans of quick and easy quilts using precut fabrics, including Jelly Rolls. Our love affair with precuts began when we were shop owners back in the '90s. Many new and exciting things were happening, like precuts! This was before fabric companies were cutting and assembling them, so shop owners had to cut their own.

So, what is a precut? It's a collection of fabrics that are cut to a specific size or shape. Since the cuts in each bundle are from the same line of fabric, they all work well together. A Jelly Roll is a delectable pack of 42 coordinated 2½" strips.

When we were cutting fat quarters and charm squares at our shop, we often had leftover fabric from the ends of the bolts. So we cut 2½" strips, rolled them into bundles, and sold them as quilt kits. Those kits were a hit! They were easy, affordable, cute, and coordinated. Customers would walk into the store and head straight toward the precuts and kits. Then the inevitable question came: What do I do with these?

The answer to that question is what led to our business today. We've designed many patterns for precuts, and in this book you'll find some of our favorite projects for Jelly Rolls. So pick a fun design, get out those pretty strips, and let's roll!

Barb Mary

Easy Log Cabin

We haven't found a quilter yet who doesn't like a Log Cabin pattern. Our version is all about color play. Diagonal rows of color really steal the show.

Finished quilt: 50½" × 60½" / Finished blocks: 10" × 10"

Materials

Yardage is based on 42"-wide fabric. Fabrics are from Hi De Ho by Me and My Sister Designs for Moda Fabrics.

- 42 strips, 2½" × 42", of assorted prints (7 yellow, 7 orange, 7 pink, 7 purple, 7 turquoise, and 7 green) for blocks*
- ¼ yard of purple print for block centers
- ½ yard of pink print for binding
- 3¼ yards of fabric for backing
- 57" × 67" piece of batting

A Moda Fabrics Jelly Roll contains 42 strips, 2½" × 42". To make the quilt as shown, you'll need 7 prints each of 6 different colors.

Cutting

All measurements include ¼" seam allowances. Keep like prints together.

From *each* of 1 yellow, 1 orange, 1 pink, 1 purple, 1 turquoise, and 1 green print strip, cut:

1 strip, 2½" × 10½" (6 total)

1 strip, 2½" × 8½" (6 total)

1 strip, 2½" × 6½" (6 total)

2 strips, 2½" × 4½" (12 total)

1 square, 2½" × 2½" (6 total)

From *each* of 1 yellow, 1 orange, 1 pink, 1 purple, 1 turquoise, and 1 green print strip, cut:

2 strips, 2½" × 8½" (12 total)

2 strips, 2½" × 6½" (12 total)

1 strip, 2½" × 4½" (6 total)

1 square, 2½" × 2½" (6 total)

From *each* of 2 yellow, 2 orange, 2 pink, 2 purple, 2 turquoise, and 2 green print strips, cut:

1 strip, 2½" × 10½" (12 total)

1 strip, 2½" × 8½" (12 total)

2 strips, 2½" × 6½" (24 total)

1 strip, 2½" × 4½" (12 total)

1 square, 2½" × 2½" (12 total)

From *each* of 1 yellow, 1 orange, 1 pink, 1 purple, 1 turquoise, and 1 green print strip, cut:

2 strips, 2½" × 8½" (12 total)

1 strip, 2½" × 6½" (6 total)

2 strips, 2½" × 4½" (12 total)

1 square, 2½" × 2½" (6 total)

From *each* of 1 yellow, 1 orange, 1 pink, 1 purple, 1 turquoise, and 1 green print strip, cut:

1 strip, 2½" × 10½" (6 total)

2 strips, 2½" × 8½" (12 total)

1 strip, 2½" × 6½" (6 total)

1 strip, 2½" × 4½" (6 total)

Continued on page 8

Continued from page 7

From *each* of 1 yellow, 1 orange, 1 pink, 1 purple, 1 turquoise, and 1 green print strip, cut:

1 strip, 2½" × 10½" (6 total)

1 strip, 2½" × 8½" (6 total)

1 strip, 2½" × 6½" (6 total)

2 strips, 2½" × 4½" (12 total)

From the purple print for block centers, cut:

2 strips, 2½" × 42"; crosscut into 30 squares, 2½" × 2½"

From the pink print, cut:

6 strips, 2¼" × 42"

Making the Blocks

Use a ¼" seam allowance and a short stitch length throughout. Press all seam allowances open.

1 Sew a yellow square to the top of a purple center square. Sew a yellow 2½" × 4½" strip to the left edge of the unit. Make five units measuring 4½" square, including seam allowances.

Make 5 units,
4½" × 4½".

2 Sew an orange 2½" × 4½" strip to the bottom of a unit. Sew an orange 2½" × 6½" strip to the right edge. Make five units measuring 6½" square, including seam allowances.

Make 5 units,
6½" × 6½".

3 Sew a yellow 2½" × 6½" strip to the top of a unit. Sew a yellow 2½" × 8½" strip to the left edge. Make five units measuring 8½" square, including seam allowances.

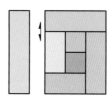

Make 5 units,
8½" × 8½".

4 Sew an orange 2½" × 8½" strip to the bottom of a unit. Sew an orange 2½" × 10½" strip to the right edge to make a block. Make five yellow and orange blocks measuring 10½" square, including seam allowances.

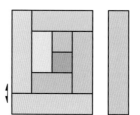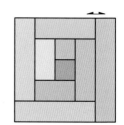

Make 5 yellow/orange blocks,
10½" × 10½".

5 Repeat steps 1–4 using orange squares and strips instead of yellow on the top and left edges of the purple center square. Use pink strips instead of orange on the bottom and right edges. Make five orange and pink blocks measuring 10½" square, including seam allowances.

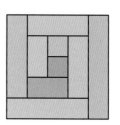

Make 5 orange/pink blocks,
10½" × 10½".

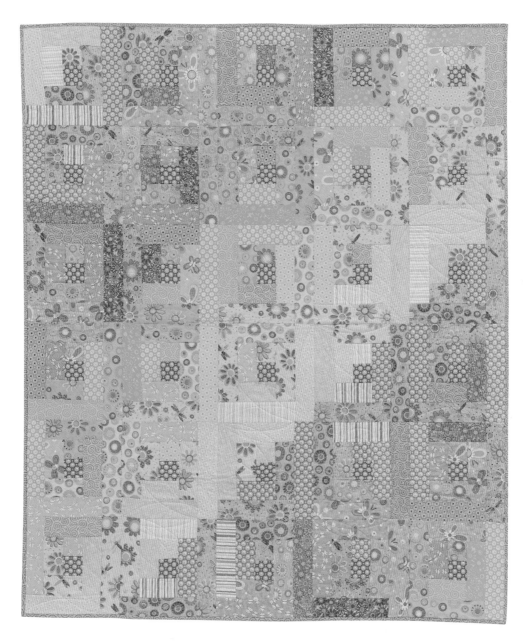

Designed by Barbara Groves and Mary Jacobson;
quilted by Sharon Elsberry

6 Repeat steps 1–4 using pink squares and strips instead of yellow on the top and left edges of the purple center square. Use purple strips instead of orange on the bottom and right edges. Make five pink and purple blocks measuring 10½" square, including seam allowances.

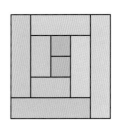

Make 5 pink/purple blocks,
10½" × 10½".

7 Repeat steps 1–4 using purple squares and strips instead of yellow on the top and left edges of the purple center square. Use turquoise strips instead of orange on the bottom and right edges. Make five purple and turquoise blocks measuring 10½" square, including seam allowances.

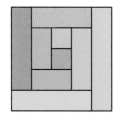

Make 5 purple/turqouise blocks,
10½" × 10½".

8 Repeat steps 1–4 using turquoise squares and strips instead of yellow on the top and left edges of the purple center square. Use green strips instead of orange on the bottom and right edges. Make five turquoise and green blocks measuring 10½" square, including seam allowances.

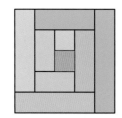

Make 5 turquoise/green blocks,
10½" × 10½".

9 Repeat steps 1–4 using green squares and strips instead of yellow on the top and left edges of the purple center square. Use yellow strips instead of orange on the bottom and right edges. Make five green and yellow blocks measuring 10½" square, including seam allowances.

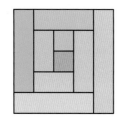

Make 5 green/yellow blocks,
10½" × 10½".

Assembling the Quilt Top

Referring to the quilt assembly diagram below, lay out the blocks in six rows of five blocks each, rotating the blocks so that the color groups form diagonal rows. Sew the block into rows, and then join the rows. The quilt top should measure 50½" × 60½".

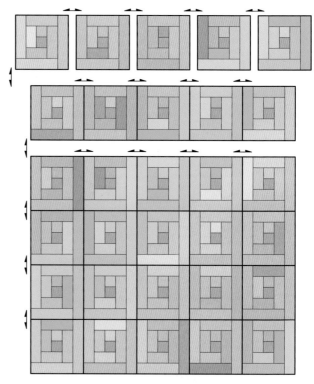

Quilt assembly

Finishing the Quilt

For more details on any finishing steps, visit ShopMartingale.com/HowtoQuilt for free downloadable information.

1 Layer the quilt top with batting and backing; baste the layers together.

2 Quilt by hand or machine. The quilt shown is machine quilted with an allover floral design.

3 Use the pink 2¼"-wide strips to make double-fold binding. Trim the excess batting and backing fabric and then attach the binding to the quilt.

Country Market

Create a clever woven look with none of the fuss. We cut our Jelly Roll strips into 6½" lengths to sew the braids. Each unit is trimmed to size in the end, so it's easy to be successful.

Finished quilt: 61¼" × 72"

Materials

Yardage is based on 42"-wide fabric. Fabrics are from Badda Bing by Me and My Sister Designs for Moda Fabrics.

- 40 strips, 2½" × 42", of assorted prints for braid strips*
- ½ yard of light print for setting triangles
- 1⅜ yards of blue check for rows and binding
- 1⅞ yards of white solid for sashing and border
- 3⅞ yards of fabric for backing
- 68" × 78" piece of batting

A Moda Fabrics Jelly Roll contains 42 strips, 2½" × 42".

Cutting

All measurements include ¼" seam allowances.

From *each* of the assorted print strips, cut:

5 strips, 2½" × 6½" (200 total)

From the light print, cut:

2 strips, 6½" × 42"; crosscut into 8 squares, 6½" × 6½". Cut in half diagonally to yield 16 triangles (1 is extra).

From the blue check, cut:

18 strips, 1½" × 42"; cut *3 of the strips* into 10 strips, 1½" × 8¾"

7 strips, 2¼" × 42"

From the white solid, cut:

7 strips, 6¼" × 42"

7 strips, 2½" × 42"

Making the Braid Columns

Use a ¼" seam allowance and a short stitch length throughout. Press all seam allowances open.

1. Divide the print 2½" × 6½" strips into five groups of 39 strips each. You'll have five strips left over for another project.

2 Using one group of strips, sew a print strip to the left short side of a light triangle. Then sew another print strip to the upper-right edge of the unit.

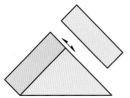 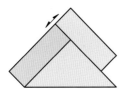

Make 1 unit.

3 Sew a print strip to the upper-left and then upper-right edges of the unit from step 2.

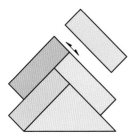 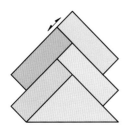

Make 1 unit.

4 Continue sewing strips to the upper-left and upper-right edges until all 39 strips in the group have been added. Note that the last strip is added to the upper-left edge.

5 Center and sew light triangles to the top of the column. Repeat the steps to make a total of five columns.

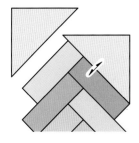 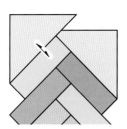

Make 5 columns.

6 Place a ruler on the long edge of a row, aligning the 45° line on the ruler with a seamline. Trim along the edge of the ruler, moving it down the length of the column. Measure 6¾" from the trimmed edge and trim the other side of the column. Repeat to trim the remaining columns to measure 6¾" wide.

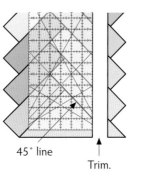 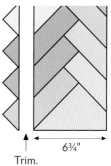

45° line   Trim.   Trim.   6¾"

7 Trim the top of each column, leaving a ¼" beyond the point on the first strip. Measure 58½" from the trimmed top edge and trim the bottom of each column. The columns should measure 6¾" × 58½", including seam allowances.

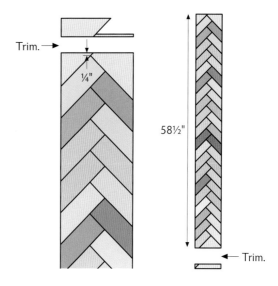

Trim. →   ¼"   58½"   ← Trim.

8 Join the remaining blue 1½"-wide strips end to end. From the pieced strip, cut 10 strips, 58½" long.

Designed by Barbara Groves and Mary Jacobson;
quilted by Sharon Elsberry

9 Sew blue 58½"-long strips to opposite sides of a braid column. Sew blue 1½" × 8¾" strips to the top and bottom edges. Make five columns measuring 8¾" × 60½", including seam allowances.

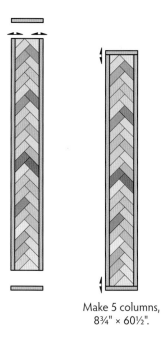

Make 5 columns,
8¾" × 60½".

strips to the top and bottom edges. The quilt top should measure 61¼" × 72".

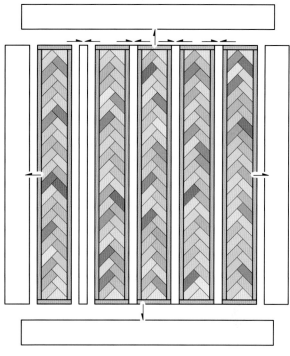

Quilt assembly

Assembling the Quilt Top

Press seam allowances in the directions indicated by the arrows.

1 Join the white 2½"-wide strips end to end. From the pieced strip, cut four 60½"-long strips.

2 Referring to the quilt assembly diagram above right, join the braid columns alternately with the white strips. The quilt center should measure 49¾" × 60½", including seam allowances.

3 Join the white 6¼"-wide strips end to end. From the pieced strip, cut two 61¼"-long strips and two 60½"-long strips. Sew the shorter strips to opposite sides of the quilt center. Sew the longer

Finishing the Quilt

For more details on any finishing steps, visit ShopMartingale.com/HowtoQuilt for free downloadable information.

1 Layer the quilt top with batting and backing; baste the layers together.

2 Quilt by hand or machine. The quilt shown is machine quilted with a swirl design in the braid columns. A design of leaves and swirls is stitched in the sashing strips and border.

3 Use the blue 2¼"-wide strips to make double-fold binding. Trim the excess batting and backing fabric and then attach the binding to the quilt.

Jelly Sandwich

Use a mix of colorful strips to create our easy "Bread" blocks—they're made of nine patches surrounded by white crusts! What a fun way to build a sandwich . . . er, quilt.

Finished quilt: 50½" × 58½"

Materials

Yardage is based on 42"-wide fabric. Fabrics are from Giggles by Me and My Sister Designs for Moda Fabrics.

- 40 strips, 2½" × 42", of assorted prints for blocks and border*
- ¾ yard of white solid for blocks
- ½ yard of green print for binding
- 3¼ yards of fabric for backing
- 57" × 65" piece of batting

A Moda Fabrics Jelly Roll contains 42 strips, 2½" × 42".

Cutting

All measurements include ¼" seam allowances.

From *1* of the assorted print strips, cut:

2 squares, 2½" × 2½"

From the white solid, cut:

14 strips, 1½" × 42"; crosscut into:

- 46 strips, 1½" × 4½"
- 46 strips, 1½" × 6½"

From the green print, cut:

6 strips, 2¼" × 42"

Making the Strip Sets

Use a ¼" seam allowance and a short stitch length throughout. Cut the strip set carefully; you won't have any leftover fabric. Press all seam allowances open.

1 Separate the remaining 39 print 2½"-wide strips into 13 sets of three strips each. We kept colors in various shades together in most cases; you'll notice a few places where we mixed colors. Sort your strips any way you like.

2 Using one set of strips, join the strips to make a strip set measuring 6½" × 42", including seam allowances. Repeat to make a total of 13 strip sets.

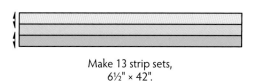

Make 13 strip sets,
6½" × 42".

3 From *one* strip set, cut two 14½"-wide segments, three 2½"-wide segments, and two 1½"-wide segments.

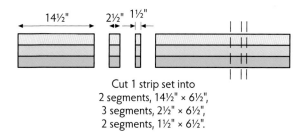

Cut 1 strip set into
2 segments, 14½" × 6½",
3 segments, 2½" × 6½",
2 segments, 1½" × 6½".

Designed by Barbara Groves and Mary Jacobson;
quilted by Sharon Elsberry

4 From *each* of four strip sets, cut one 14½"-wide segment, one 12½"-wide segment, four 2½"-wide segments, and two 1½"-wide segments.

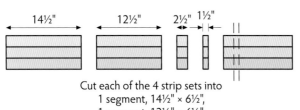

Cut each of the 4 strip sets into
1 segment, 14½" × 6½",
1 segment, 12½" × 6½",
4 segments, 2½" × 6½",
2 segments, 1½" × 6½".

5 From *each* of four strip sets, cut one 14½"-wide segment, one 8½"-wide segment, four 2½"-wide segments, and three 1½"-wide segments.

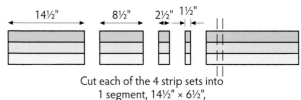

Cut each of the 4 strip sets into
1 segment, 14½" × 6½",
1 segment, 8½" × 6½",
4 segments, 2½" × 6½",
3 segments, 1½" × 6½".

6 From *each* of the four remaining strip sets, cut one 14½"-wide segment, six 2½"-wide segments, and six 1½"-wide segments.

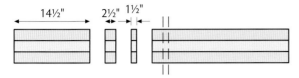

Cut each of the 4 strip sets into
1 segment, 14½" × 6½",
6 segments, 2½" × 6½",
6 segments, 1½" × 6½".

including seam allowances. The remaining 2½"-wide segments will be used to make the pieced border.

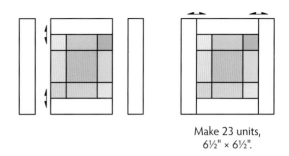

Make 23 units,
6½" × 6½".

Making the Bread Blocks

1 Lay out two random 1½"-wide segments and one 2½"-wide segment as shown. Join the segments to make a unit measuring 6½" × 4½", including seam allowances. Make 23 units.

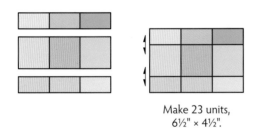

Make 23 units,
6½" × 4½".

2 Trim 1" from each side of a unit from step 1. Make 23 units measuring 4½" square, including seam allowances.

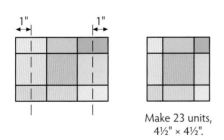

Make 23 units,
4½" × 4½".

3 Sew white 1½" × 4½" strips to the top and bottom edges of a unit from step 2. Sew white 1½" × 6½" strips to opposite sides of the unit to make a block. Make 23 blocks measuring 6½" square,

Assembling the Quilt Top

1 Join three blocks and two 14½"-wide segments to make row A. Make five rows measuring 6½" × 46½", including seam allowances.

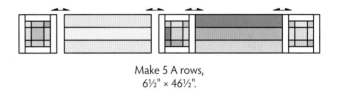

Make 5 A rows,
6½" × 46½".

2 Join two blocks, one 8½"-wide segment, one 14½"-wide segment, and one 12½"-wide segment to make row B. Make two rows measuring 6½" × 46½", including seam allowances.

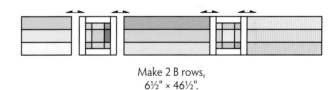

Make 2 B rows,
6½" × 46½".

3 Join two blocks, one 12½"-wide segment, one 14½"-wide segment, and one 8½"-wide segment to make row C. Make two rows measuring 6½" × 46½", including seam allowances.

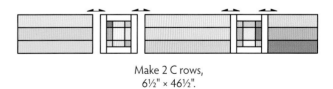

Make 2 C rows,
6½" × 46½".

4 Lay out the A–C rows as shown in the quilt assembly diagram. Join the rows to make the quilt center, which should measure 46½" × 54½", including seam allowances.

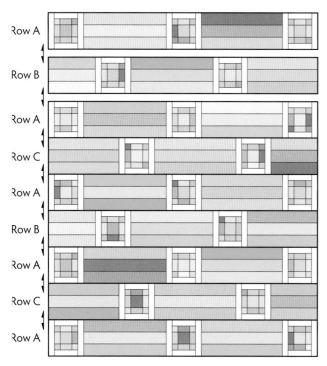

Row A

Row B

Row A

Row C

Row A

Row B

Row A

Row C

Row A

Quilt assembly

5 Join nine 2½"-wide segments end to end to make a side border measuring 2½" × 54½", including seam allowances. Make two. Join eight 2½"-wide segments and one 2½" square to make a top border measuring 2½" × 50½", including seam allowances. Repeat to make the bottom border. Press all seam allowances open. You'll have two segments left over.

Make 2 side borders,
2½" × 54½".

Make 2 top/bottom borders,
2½" × 50½".

6 Sew the borders to opposite sides of the quilt top and then to the top and bottom edges. The quilt top should measure 50½" × 58½".

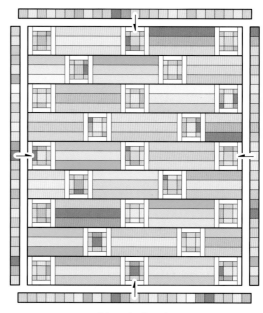

Adding the borders

Finishing the Quilt

For more details on any finishing steps, visit ShopMartingale.com/HowtoQuilt for free downloadable information.

1 Layer the quilt top with batting and backing; baste the layers together.

2 Quilt by hand or machine. The quilt shown is machine quilted with an allover design of hearts, leaves, and flowers.

3 Use the green 2¼"-wide strips to make double-fold binding. Trim the excess batting and backing fabric and then attach the binding to the quilt.

Strawberry Lemonade

Don't these blocks look like little gift boxes all wrapped up with a ribbon and a white bow on top? No matter what colors you choose, this pattern will be a delight to piece.

Finished quilt: 59½" × 67¼" / Finished blocks: 5½" × 5½"

Materials

Yardage is based on 42"-wide fabric. Fabrics are from Strawberry Lemonade by Me and My Sister Designs for Moda Fabrics.

- 40 strips, 2½" × 42", of assorted prints for blocks*
- ⅝ yard of white solid for blocks
- ⅝ yard of light print for setting triangles
- ½ yard of yellow print for inner border
- 1 yard of pink dot for outer border
- ½ yard of pink print for binding
- 3¾ yards of fabric for backing
- 66" × 74" piece of batting

*A Moda Fabrics Jelly Roll contains 42 strips, 2½" × 42".

Cutting

All measurements include ¼" seam allowances. Cut the assorted print strips carefully; you won't have any leftover fabric.

From *each* of the assorted print strips, cut:

2 strips, 2½" × 13½" (80 total)

2 strips, 1¼" × 13½" (80 total)

From the white solid, cut:

8 strips, 2" × 42"; crosscut into 160 squares, 2" × 2"

From the light print, cut:

2 strips, 10" × 42"; crosscut into:

- 6 squares, 10" × 10"; cut into quarters diagonally to yield 24 side triangles (2 are extra)
- 2 squares, 5" × 5"; cut in half diagonally to yield 4 corner triangles

From the yellow print, cut:

6 strips, 2½" × 42"

From the pink dot, cut:

7 strips, 4½" × 42"

From the pink print, cut:

7 strips, 2¼" × 42"

Making the Blocks

Use a ¼" seam allowance and a short stitch length throughout. Press all seam allowances open.

1 Pair each print 2½" × 13½" strip with a contrasting print 1¼" × 13½" strip to make 80 pairs.

2 Join each pair of strips to make a strip set measuring 3¼" × 13½", including seam allowances. Make 80 strip sets. Cut each strip set into four 3¼"-wide segments (320 total). As you cut, keep like segments together.

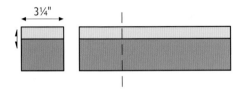

Make 80 strip sets, 3¼" × 13½".
Cut 320 segments, 3¼" × 3¼".

3 Draw a diagonal line from corner to corner on the wrong side of the white 2" squares. Place a marked square on one corner of a segment from step 2, right sides together, noting the direction of the marked line. Sew on the marked line. Trim the excess corner fabric ¼" from the stitched line. Repeat to make 80 pairs of matching units (160 total) measuring 3¼" square, including seam allowances.

Make 80 pairs of matching units, 3¼" × 3¼".

4 Using matching segments and units, lay out two segments from step 2 and two units from step 3 in two rows. Sew the pieces into rows. Join the rows to make a block measuring 6" square, including seam allowances. Make 80 blocks. You'll have eight extra blocks.

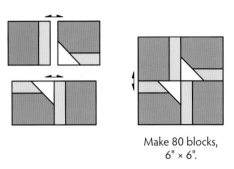

Make 80 blocks, 6" × 6".

Assembling the Quilt Top

When adding borders, press seam allowances away from the quilt center.

1 Referring to the quilt assembly diagram, arrange and sew the blocks and light print side triangles together in diagonal rows. Join the rows, adding the light print corner triangles last.

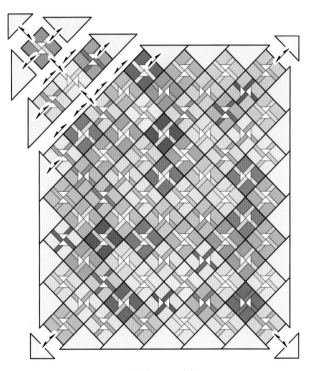

Quilt assembly

Designed by Barbara Groves and Mary Jacobson;
quilted by Sharon Elsberry

2 Trim and square up the quilt top, making sure to leave ½" beyond the points of all blocks for seam allowances. The quilt center should measure 47½" × 55¼", including seam allowances.

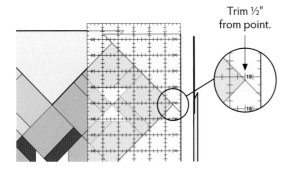

Trim ½" from point.

3 Join the yellow 2½"-wide strips end to end. From the pieced strip, cut two 55¼"-long strips and two 51½"-long strips. Sew the longer strips to opposite sides of the quilt center. Sew the shorter strips to the top and bottom edges. The quilt top should measure 51½" × 59¼", including seam allowances.

4 Join the pink dot 4½"-wide strips end to end. From the pieced strip, cut two 59¼"-long strips and two 59½"-long strips. Sew the 59¼"-long strips to opposite sides of the quilt center. Sew the 59½"-long strips to the top and bottom edges. The quilt top should measure 59½" × 67¼".

Finishing the Quilt

For more details on any finishing steps, visit ShopMartingale.com/HowtoQuilt for free downloadable information.

1 Layer the quilt top with batting and backing; baste the layers together.

2 Quilt by hand or machine. The quilt shown is machine quilted with an allover design of large swirls.

3 Use the pink print 2¼"-wide strips to make double-fold binding. Trim the excess batting and backing fabric and then attach the binding to the quilt.

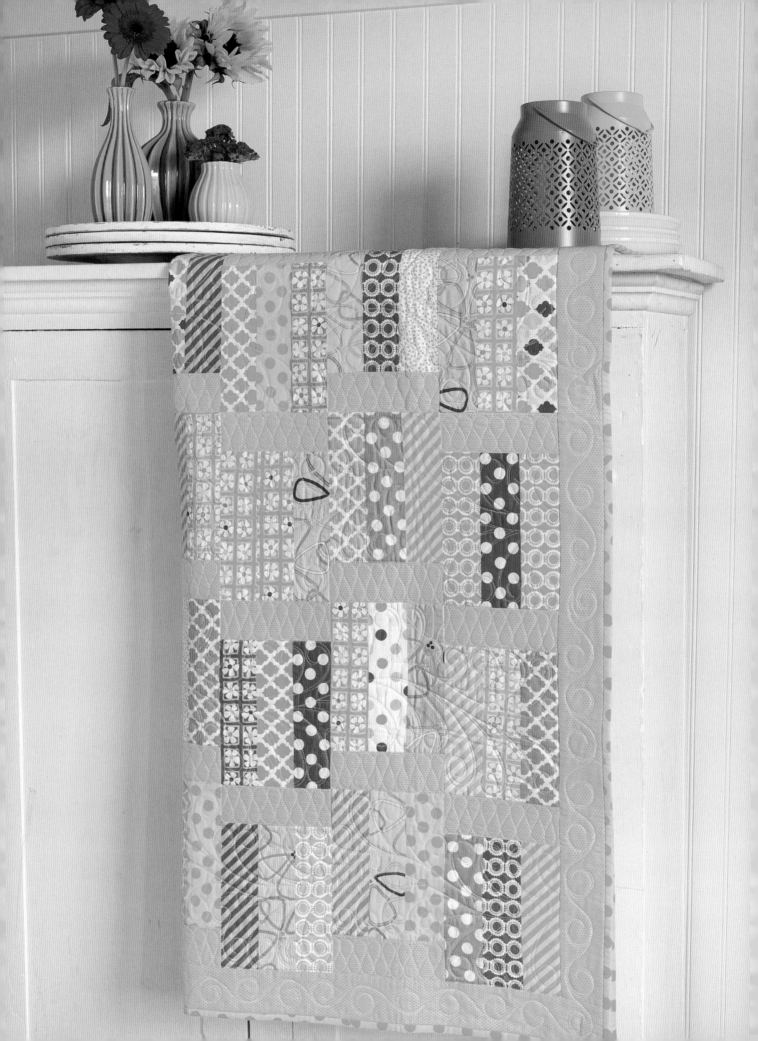

Chart Topper

True confession: we didn't like bar charts in math class. But when you make them out of fabric, they make your heart skip a beat—in a good way!

Finished quilt: 46½" × 61½" / Finished blocks: 6" × 9½"

Materials

Yardage is based on 42"-wide fabric. Fabrics are from Grow by Me and My Sister Designs for Moda Fabrics.

- 26 strips, 2½ × 42", of assorted prints for blocks*
- 1 yard of turquoise print for blocks and border
- ½ yard of turquoise dot for binding
- 3 yards of fabric for backing
- 53" × 68" piece of batting

A Moda Fabrics Jelly Roll contains 42 strips, 2½" × 42".

Cutting

All measurements include ¼" seam allowances.

From each of the assorted print strips, cut:

5 strips, 2½" × 8" (130 total; 4 are extra)

From the turquoise print, cut:

13 strips, 2½" × 42"; crosscut 7 of the strips into 42 strips, 2½" × 6½"

From the turquoise dot, cut:

6 strips, 2¼" × 42"

Making the Blocks

Use a ¼" seam allowance and a short stitch length throughout. Press all seam allowances open.

1 Sew three different-print strips side by side to make a strip unit measuring 6½" × 8", including seam allowances. Make 42 units.

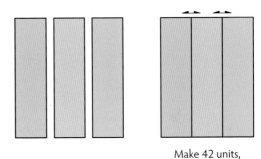

Make 42 units, 6½" × 8".

2 Sew a turquoise print 2½" × 6½" strip to the top of a strip unit to make a block. Make 42 blocks measuring 6½" × 10", including seam allowances.

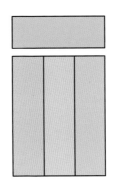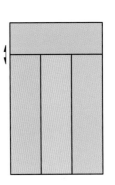

Make 42 units, 6½" × 10".

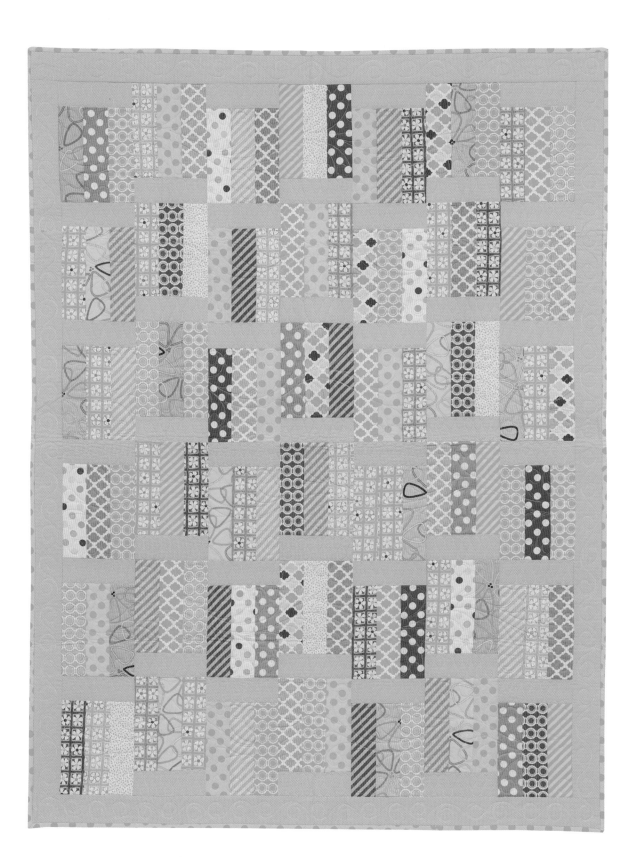

Designed by Barbara Groves and Mary Jacobson;
quilted by Sharon Elsberry

Assembling the Quilt Top

1 Referring to the quilt assembly diagram below, lay out the blocks in six rows of seven blocks each, rotating every other block as shown. Sew the blocks into rows. Join the rows to make the quilt center. The quilt center should measure 42½" × 57½", including seam allowances.

2 Join the remaining turquoise print 2½"-wide strips end to end. From the pieced strip, cut two 57½"-long strips and two 46½"-long strips. Sew the longer strips to opposite sides of the quilt center. Sew the shorter strips to the top and bottom edges. The quilt top should measure 46½" × 61½".

Finishing the Quilt

For more details on any finishing steps, visit ShopMartingale.com/HowtoQuilt for free downloadable information.

1 Layer the quilt top with batting and backing; baste the layers together.

2 Quilt by hand or machine. The quilt shown is machine quilted with a large swirl design in the print strips. Ribbon candy and swirls are stitched in the turquoise strips.

3 Use the turquoise dot 2¼"-wide strips to make double-fold binding. Trim the excess batting and backing fabric and then attach the binding to the quilt.

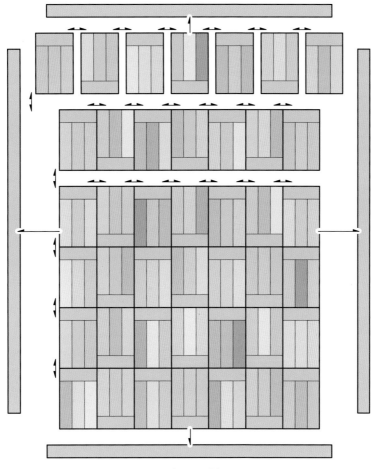

Quilt assembly

Chain Links

Simple squares and rectangles cut from 2½" strips are all you need to piece this easier-than-it-looks design. The top is assembled in rows rather than blocks, for a fun twin-size quilt.

Finished quilt: 72½" × 84½"

Materials

Yardage is based on 42"-wide fabric. Fabrics are from Brighten Up by Me and My Sister Designs for Moda Fabrics.

- 40 strips, 2½" × 42", of assorted prints for *chain* links*
- 3½ yards of white solid for chain links, sashing, and border
- ⅔ yard of purple print for binding
- 6¾ yards of fabric for backing**
- 81" × 93" piece of batting

*A Moda Fabrics Jelly Roll contains 42 strips, 2½"×42".

**If your fabric is at least 43" wide, 5¼ yards will be enough.

Cutting

All measurements include ¼" seam allowances. Keep like prints together.

From *each* of the assorted print strips, cut:

6 strips, 2½" × 6½" (240 total)

From the white solid, cut:

33 strips, 2½" × 42"; crosscut *18 of the strips* into:

- 210 squares, 2½" × 2½"
- 30 pieces, 2½" × 4½"

8 strips, 3½" × 42"

From the purple print, cut:

9 strips, 2¼" × 42"

Assembling the Quilt Top

Use a ¼" seam allowance and a short stitch length throughout. Press all seam allowances open.

1 This quilt is constructed in rows. For each row, you'll need:

- 6 strips, 2½" × 6½", from four different prints (24 total)
- 21 white 2½" squares
- 3 white 2½" × 4½" pieces

2 Lay out the print strips and white squares and pieces in three rows as shown. Sew into three pieced strips. Join the strips to make a row. Make 10 rows measuring 6½" × 66½", including seam allowances.

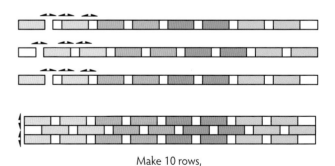

Make 10 rows,
6½" × 66½".

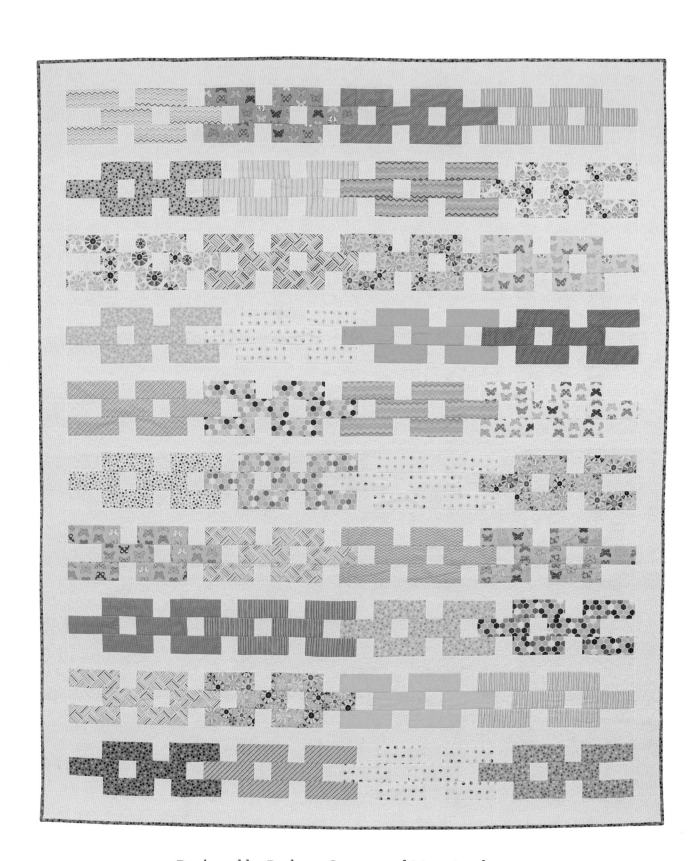

Designed by Barbara Groves and Mary Jacobson;
quilted by Sharon Elsberry

3 Join the remaining white 2½"-wide strips end to end. From the pieced strip, cut nine sashing strips, 2½" × 66½".

4 Referring to the quilt assembly diagram below, lay out the rows from step 2 alternately with the white sashing strips, rotating every other row 180°. Join the rows and strips to make the quilt center, which should measure 66½" × 78½", including seam allowances.

5 Join the white 3½"-wide strips end to end. From the pieced strip, cut two 78½"-long strips and two 72½"-long strips. Sew the longer strips to opposite sides of the quilt center. Sew the shorter strips to the top and bottom edges. The quilt top should measure 72½" × 84½".

Finishing the Quilt

For more details on any finishing steps, visit ShopMartingale.com/HowtoQuilt for free downloadable information.

1 Layer the quilt top with batting and backing; baste the layers together.

2 Quilt by hand or machine. The quilt shown is machine quilted with an allover design of swirls and spirals.

3 Use the purple 2¼"-wide strips to make double-fold binding. Trim the excess batting and backing fabric and then attach the binding to the quilt.

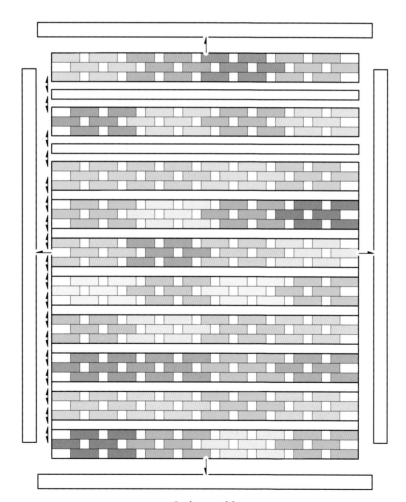

Quilt assembly

Starburst

Each ray of this shining star is made using stitch-and-flip corners. This easy method makes it a snap to create a unique design that no one will guess started out as Jelly Roll strips!

Finished quilt: 54½" × 62½

Materials

Yardage is based on 42"-wide fabric. Fabrics are from Grow by Me and My Sister Designs for Moda Fabrics.

- 40 strips, 2½" × 42", of assorted prints for blocks*
- 2⅛ yards of white solid for blocks, setting, and sashing
- ½ yard of purple diagonal stripe for binding
- 3½ yards of fabric for backing
- 61" × 69" piece of batting

A Moda Fabrics Jelly Roll contains 42 strips, 2½" × 42".

Cutting

All measurements include ¼" seam allowances. Keep like prints together.

From *each* of the assorted print strips, cut:

4 strips, 2½" × 7" (160 total)

4 squares, 2½" × 2½" (160 total)

From the white solid, cut:

10 strips, 2½" × 42"; crosscut into 160 squares, 2½" × 2½"

6 strips, 4½" × 42"; crosscut into:
- 8 strips, 4½" × 12½"
- 8 pieces, 4½" × 8½"
- 8 squares, 4½" × 4½"
- 2 pieces, 3½" × 4½"
- 2 pieces, 1½" × 4½"

1 strip, 13½" × 42"; crosscut into 4 pieces, 9½" × 13½"

From the purple diagonal stripe, cut:

7 strips, 2¼" × 42"

Making the Blocks

Use a ¼" seam allowance and a short stitch length throughout. Press all seam allowances open.

1 For each block, you'll need:
- 4 matching print 2½" × 7" strips
- 4 matching coordinating print 2½" squares
- 4 white 2½" squares

2 Draw a diagonal line from corner to corner on the wrong side of the print and white 2½" squares.

3 Place a marked white square on the left end of a print strip, right sides together. Place a marked print square on the right end of the print strip. Note the orientation of the marked lines. Sew on the marked lines. Trim the excess corner fabric ¼" from the stitched lines. Make two units measuring 2½" × 7", including seam allowances.

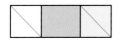 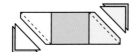

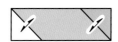

Make 2 units,
2½" × 7".

4 Place a marked print square on the left end of a print strip, right sides together. Place a marked white square on the right end of the print strip. Make sure to reverse the orientation of the marked lines. Sew on the marked lines. Trim the excess corner fabric ¼" from the stitched lines. Make two reversed units measuring 2½" × 7", including seam allowances.

 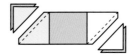

Make 2 reversed units,
2½" × 7".

5 Lay out the units from steps 3 and 4 in two rows of two as shown. Sew the units into rows. Join the rows to make a block measuring 4½" × 13½", including seam allowances. Repeat the steps to make 40 blocks.

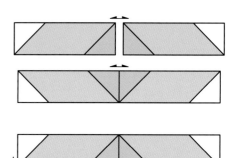

Make 40 blocks,
4½" × 13½".

Assembling the Quilt Top

The quilt-top center is assembled in sections. Make a total of four sections.

1 Sew a block to the right edge of a white 9½" × 13½" piece. Sew a block to the bottom of the unit. The unit should measure 13½" × 17½", including seam allowances.

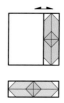

Make 1 unit,
13½" × 17½".

Designed by Barbara Groves and Mary Jacobson;
quilted by Sharon Elsberry

2 Sew a white 4½" square to one end of a block. Make two units measuring 4½" × 17½". Sew the units to the right edge first and then the bottom of the unit from step 1. The unit should measure 17½" × 21½", including seam allowances.

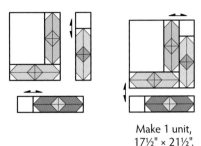

Make 1 unit,
17½" × 21½".

3 Sew a white 4½" × 8½" piece to one end of a block. Make two units measuring 4½" × 21½". Sew the units to the right edge first and then the bottom of the unit from step 2. The unit should measure 21½" × 25½", including seam allowances.

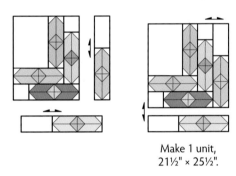

Make 1 unit,
21½" × 25½".

4 Sew a white 4½" × 12½" strip to one end of a block. Make two units measuring 4½" × 25½". Sew the units to the right edge and then the bottom of the unit to make a section. Make two sections measuring 25½" × 29½", including seam allowances.

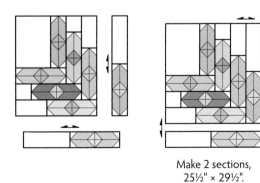

Make 2 sections,
25½" × 29½".

5 Repeat steps 1–4 to sew white pieces to the blocks. Referring to the diagrams, join the blocks, units, and white 9½" × 13½" piece to make a reversed section. Make two sections measuring 25½" × 29½", including seam allowances.

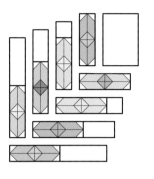
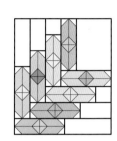

Make 2 sections,
25½" × 29½".

6 Join one white 3½" × 4½" piece and two blocks to make a vertical sashing strip. Make two strips measuring 4½" × 29½", including seam allowances.

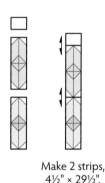

Make 2 strips,
4½" × 29½".

7 Join two white 1½" × 4½" pieces and four blocks to make a horizontal sashing strip measuring 4½" × 54½", including seam allowances.

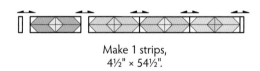

Make 1 strips,
4½" × 54½".

8 Referring to the quilt assembly diagram below, lay out the sections, vertical sashing strips, and horizontal sashing strip in three rows, rotating the bottom sections and vertical strips as shown. Sew the sections and vertical strips into rows. Join the rows and horizontal strip. The quilt top should measure 54½" × 62½".

Finishing the Quilt

For more details on any finishing steps, visit ShopMartingale.com/HowtoQuilt for free downloadable information.

1 Layer the quilt top with batting and backing; baste the layers together.

2 Quilt by hand or machine. The quilt shown is machine quilted with curved lines in the blocks. A large floral design is stitched in the white background.

3 Use the purple 2¼"-wide strips to make double-fold binding. Trim the excess batting and backing fabric and then attach the binding to the quilt.

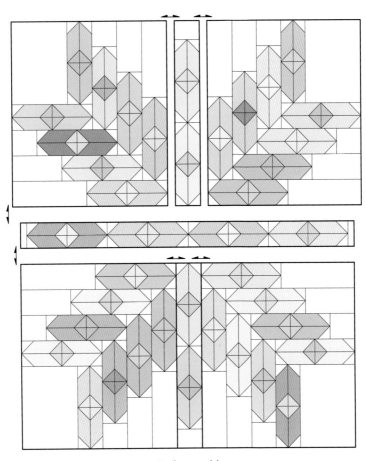

Quilt assembly

Rainbow Connection

We sewed our strips into pretty links and joined them end to end. When you place similar colors in a row, you can arrange the rows to make your own beautiful Rainbow Connection.

Finished quilt: 72½" × 82½ / Finished blocks: 6" × 17"

Materials

Yardage is based on 42"-wide fabric. Fabrics are from Hi De Ho by Me and My Sister Designs for Moda Fabrics.

- 40 strips, 2½" × 42", of assorted prints for blocks *
- 3⅝ yards of white solid for blocks
- ⅔ yard of purple print for binding
- 6¾ yards of fabric for backing**
- 81" × 91" piece of batting

A Moda Fabrics Jelly Roll contains 42 strips, 2½" × 42".

**If your fabric is at least 43" wide, 5⅛ yards will be enough.*

Cutting

All measurements include ¼" seam allowances. Cut the assorted print strips carefully; you won't have any leftover fabric. Keep like prints together.

From each of the assorted print strips, cut:

2 strips, 2½" × 13½" (80 total)

2 strips, 2½" × 6½" (80 total)

From the white solid, cut:

3 strips, 13½" × 42"; crosscut into 40 strips, 2½" × 13½"

24 strips, 2½" × 42"

8 strips, 2" × 42"; crosscut into 160 squares, 2" × 2"

From the purple print, cut:

9 strips, 2¼" × 42"

Making the Blocks

Use a ¼" seam allowance and a short stitch length throughout. Press all seam allowances open.

1 For each block, you'll need:

- 2 matching print 2½" × 13½" strips
- 2 matching print 2½" × 6½" strips
- 1 white 2½" × 13½" strip
- 4 white 2" squares

2 Sew a print 2½" × 13½" strip to each long side of a white strip to make a center unit measuring 6½" × 13½", including seam allowances.

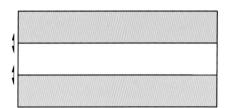

Make 1 unit,
6½" × 13½".

41

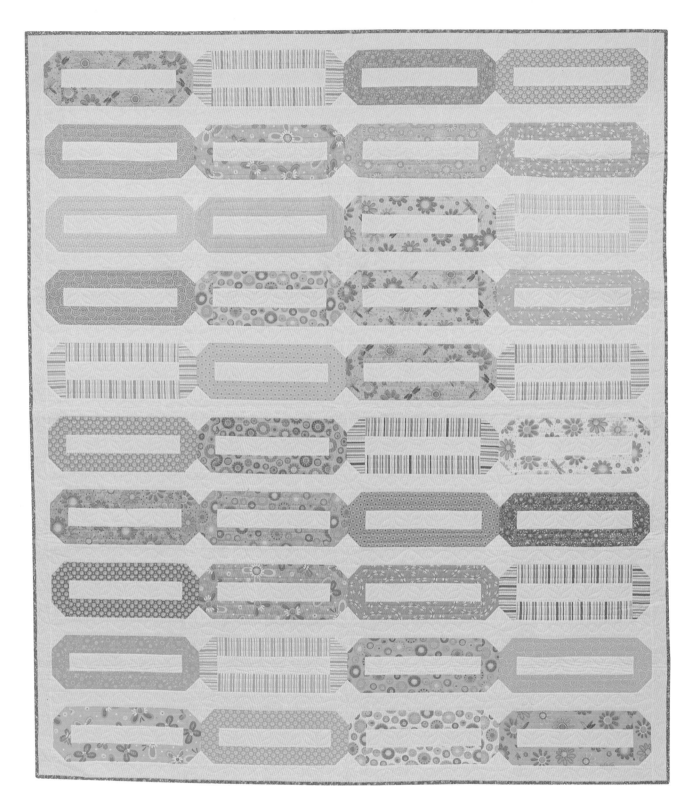

Designed by Barbara Groves and Mary Jacobson;
quilted by Sharon Elsberry

3 Draw a diagonal line from corner to corner on the wrong side of the white 2" squares. Place marked squares on adjacent corners of a print 2½" × 6½" strip. Sew on the marked lines. Trim the excess corner fabric, ¼" from the stitched lines. Make one end unit and one reversed end unit. The units should measure 2½" × 6½", including seam allowances.

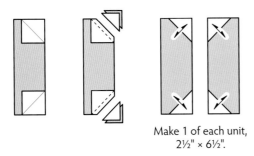

Make 1 of each unit,
2½" × 6½".

4 Join the end units and center unit to make a block measuring 6½" × 17½", including seam allowances. Make 40 blocks.

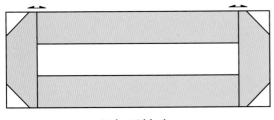

Make 40 blocks,
6½" × 17½".

Assembling the Quilt Top

When adding sashing and borders, press seam allowances in the directions indicated by the arrows.

1 Referring to the quilt assembly diagram above right, lay out the blocks in 10 rows of four blocks each. Notice that in the quilt on page 42, the blocks are arranged by color. Join the blocks in each row. Make 10 rows measuring 6½" × 68½", including seam allowances.

2 Join the white 2½"-wide strips end to end. From the pieced strip, cut nine 68½"-long sashing strips, two 78½"-long strips, and two 72½"-long strips.

3 Join the block rows alternately with the white 68½"-long sashing strips to make

the quilt center. The quilt center should measure 68½" × 78½", including seam allowances.

4 Sew the white 78½"-long strips to opposite sides of the quilt center. Sew the white 72½"-long strips to the top and bottom edges. The quilt top should measure 72½" × 82½".

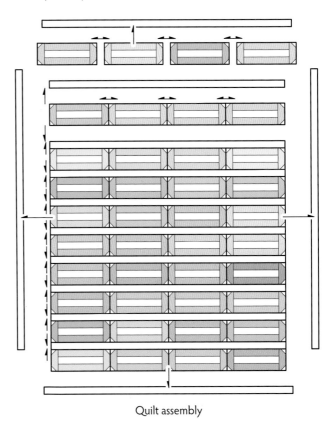

Quilt assembly

Finishing the Quilt

For more details on any finishing steps, visit ShopMartingale.com/HowtoQuilt for free downloadable information.

1 Layer the quilt top with batting and backing; baste the layers together.

2 Quilt by hand or machine. The quilt shown is machine quilted with leaves in the block centers and straight lines in the prints. A flower motif and swirls are stitched in the white sashing strips and border.

3 Use the purple 2¼"-wide strips to make double-fold binding. Trim the excess batting and backing fabric and then attach the binding to the quilt.

A-Mazing

Mix and match quarter Log Cabin blocks for a true riot of color. The blocks are easy to piece and arranging them to complete your quilt top is all part of the fun.

Finished quilt: 52½" × 52½" / Finished blocks: 16" × 16"

Materials

Yardage is based on 42"-wide fabric. Fabrics are from Confetti by Me and My Sister Designs for Moda Fabrics.

- 36 strips, 2½" × 42", of assorted prints for blocks *
- ½ yard of white solid for border
- ½ yard of turquoise stripe for binding
- 3⅜ yard of fabric for backing
- 59" × 59" piece of batting

A Moda Fabrics Jelly Roll contains 42 strips, 2½"×42".

Cutting

All measurements include ¼" seam allowances. Keep like prints together.

From *each* of the assorted print strips, cut:

1 strip, 2½" × 28" (36 total)

1 strip, 2½" × 8½" (36 total)

From the white solid, cut:

6 strips, 2½" × 42"

From the turquoise stripe, cut:

6 strips, 2¼" × 42"

Making the Blocks

Use a ¼" seam allowance and a short stitch length throughout. Press all seam allowances open.

1   Divide the print strips into 18 sets of two contrasting prints.

2   Using the strips from one set, join the 2½" × 28" strips to make a strip set measuring 4½" × 28", including seam allowances. Make a total of 18 strip sets. Cut each strip set into two 2½" × 4½" segments, two 4½" × 4½" segments, and two 4½" × 6½" segments.

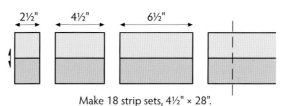

Make 18 strip sets, 4½" × 28".
Cut each strip set into
2 segments, 2½" × 4½",
2 segments, 4½" × 4½",
2 segments, 4½" × 6½".

Designed by Barbara Groves and Mary Jacobson;
quilted by Sharon Elsberry

3 Using the segments from one strip set, lay out one 2½" × 4½" segment, one 4½" × 4½" segment, one 4½" × 6½" segment, and one matching 2½" × 8½" strip, noting the orientation of the segments. Join the segments, and then add the 2½" × 8½" strip to the left edge. The quarter-block

unit should measure 8½" square, including seam allowances.

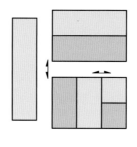 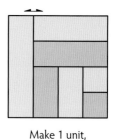

Make 1 unit,
8½" × 8½".

4 Lay out the remaining segments from the same strip set and the matching 2½" × 8½" strip, reversing the orientation of the segments. Join the segments, and then add the strip to the left edge. The quarter-block unit should measure 8½" square, including seam allowances.

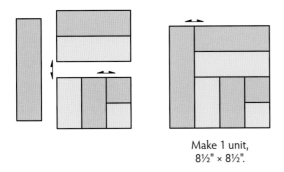

Make 1 unit,
8½" × 8½".

5 Repeat steps 2 and 3 to make a total of 36 quarter-block units.

6 Lay out four quarter-block units in two rows of two. Sew the units into rows. Join the rows to make a block. Make nine blocks measuring 16½" square, including seam allowances.

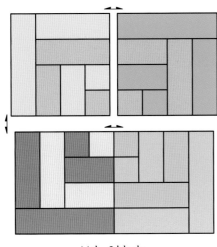

Make 9 blocks,
16½" × 16½".

Assembling the Quilt Top

1 Referring to the quilt assembly diagram above right, lay out the blocks in three rows of three blocks each. Sew the blocks into rows and then join the rows. The quilt center should measure 48½" square, including seam allowances.

2 Join the white 2½"-wide strips end to end. From the pieced strip, cut two 52½"-long strips and two 48½"-long strips. Sew the shorter strips to opposite sides of the quilt top. Sew the longer strips to the top and bottom edges. The quilt top should measure 52½" square.

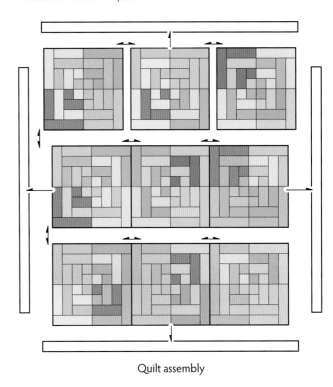

Quilt assembly

Finishing the Quilt

For more details on any finishing steps, visit ShopMartingale.com/HowtoQuilt for free downloadable information.

1 Layer the quilt top with batting and backing; baste the layers together.

2 Quilt by hand or machine. The quilt shown is machine quilted with curved lines and a pumpkin seed motif in the blocks. A flower motif is stitched in the border.

3 Use the turquoise 2¼"-wide strips to make double-fold binding. Trim the excess batting and backing fabric and then attach the binding to the quilt.

About the Authors

Sisters Barbara Groves and Mary Jacobson make up the popular design team of Me and My Sister Designs, based in Tempe, Arizona. Their belief in fast, fun, and easy designs can be seen in the quilts created for their pattern company, in their books, and in their fabric designs for Moda. To learn more, visit the authors at MeandMySisterDesigns.com.